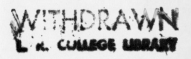

The Chimeras

Gerard de Nerval

Nerval

The Chimeras

translated by Peter Jay

Essays by Richard Holmes
and Peter Jay

BLACK SWAN BOOKS

First edition

Published by

BLACK SWAN BOOKS Ltd.
P.O. Box 327
Redding Ridge, CT 06876

ISBN 0-933806-34-5

Printed in England

TO CAROLINE ROOT

Un mystère d'amour dans le métal repose

La femme est la Chimère de l'homme
ou son démon, comme vous voudrez . . .

Contents

Preface

GÉRARD DE NERVAL's sonnets first appeared as a group entitled *Les Chimères* in January 1854, when they were appended to *Les Filles du Feu*. It seems that Nerval worked on the poems over a period of eleven years, from 1843; he had kept them largely private while pursuing his public career of playwright and literary journalist. The poems were not arranged in their final order until late in 1853, when Nerval was busily supervising new editions of his work. Earlier that year the "Le Christ aux Oliviers" poems, together with "Vers Dorés" and "Delfica", had appeared as a group with the title *Mysticisme*. (The "Christ" sequence had already been published separately, in 1844.) There are both manuscript and printed versions of several sonnets which combine the quatrains and tercets from different poems; one, for example, takes the first eight lines of "Myrtho" and the last six of "Delfica", while with small variants another consists of the opening of "Delfica" and the ending of "Myrtho". Significantly, this is titled "à J—y Colonna", i.e. Jenny Colon, the actress whom he loved unrequitedly, and who died in June 1842.

The poems, then, were chimerical in their composition. Their publication together in 1854 must imply that Nerval then intended them to be read as a single work; perhaps, too, in the light of the prose stories and essay which precede them in *Les Filles du Feu*, or as a summation of his work. Even if we now take the poems out of that context—as has become customary—an intuitive logic can be sensed in their order. It seems essential to the spirit of the cycle that it should close with "Vers Dorés".

The "difficulty" of the poems has become legendary. Nerval himself had this to say of them: "They are hardly more obscure than Hegel's metaphysics or Swedenborg's *Memorabilia*; and would lose their spell by being explained,

9

if such a thing were possible." Although the poems offer scholars and biographers a rich field for speculation, their strange and compelling artistic alchemy leaves their mystery unscathed by the onslaught of analysis to which they have been subjected.

In his essay on Nerval, reprinted in *The Symbolist Movement in Literature* (1899), Arthur Symons wrote that the poems are "a kind of miracle, which may be held to have created something at least of the method of the later Symbolists." This much seems indisputable. They were composed, Nerval tells us, "in that state of meditation which the Germans would call *supernaturalist.*" The poems pick up themes, ideas and images from his prose fiction, including his "travel" writings, and from what one might call the fiction of his own biography (Nerval once wrote that he liked to arrange his life like a novel). Symbolic images such as the black sun, the star and the girl with the hollyhock occur in *Aurélia*; the girl biting lemons appears in *Octavie*, and so on.

"Few writers, I think," says Norma Rinsler in her study of the poems, "can have produced a body of work in which the separate items are so closely related to each other . . . In effect, Nerval wrote only one work, which is essentially the story of his life, 'l'histoire du cœur d'un grand poète'; every part of it sheds some light on every other part." Yet the charged clarity of the poems lifts them to a higher artistic level than anything else he wrote. Actual and imagined experience are inseparably mingled and transfigured in the poems; their greatness is a peculiar combination of a graceful lightness of touch and a purposeful gravity—qualities apparent, I think, even to non-native readers or those whose French is as moderate as mine.

On the vexed question of the complexity of the mythological references, I concluded that brief notes or glosses would very likely be more misleading than none. They would necessarily be perfunctory, reductive. Fortunately the interested reader can pursue these things in depth in Norma Rinsler's elegant and imaginative commentary, *Gérard de Nerval: Les Chimères* (1973), easily available in the Athlone French Poets series. She has also published in the same series a monograph, *Gérard de Nerval* (1973), which covers the rest of his career and writings. My debt to Dr Rinsler's work is enormous. An older but still useful and informative text with commentary in French is Jeanine Moulin's *Les Chimères* in the Textes Littéraires Français series (Librairie Droz, 1949 and reprinted).

The origins of this version go back to 1966. Perhaps only one line, the sixth of "Myrtho", has survived unaltered from those first stumbling drafts. Sometime around 1978 the versions began to take shape, prompted largely by Richard Holmes's unpublished work on Nerval. I am grateful to him, to Harry Guest and to Norma Rinsler for their generous and careful comments on my drafts, and to Michael Schmidt for printing the versions, in a slightly earlier form, in *PN Review*.

Although the translation faces the French text here, it is not intended to provide the sort of word-for-word, or phrase-by-phrase, correspondence to which a literal prose translation might aspire. (I know, for example, that *mille* "means" thousand, not million.) While I hope to have avoided misconstruing his beautifully lucid and syntactically simple French, my aim has been, like Nerval's in his versions from German poetry, to restate the poems as whole poems, to turn *Les Chimères* into *The Chimeras*—a chimerical task, if there ever was one!—and to return the reader through them to the better understanding of *le bon Gérard*'s poetic genius, which itself serves and honours the universal life embodied in his vision. "La vie d'un poète est celle de tous", as he wrote; and again, "l'expérience de chacun est le trésor de tous."

PETER JAY

Oxford, March 1981 – Greenwich, June 1984

LES CHIMÈRES
THE CHIMERAS

El Desdichado

Je suis le ténébreux,—le veuf,—l'inconsolé,
Le prince d'Aquitaine à la tour abolie:
Ma seule *étoile* est morte,—et mon luth constellé
Porte le *Soleil noir* de la *Mélancolie.*

Dans la nuit du tombeau, toi qui m'as consolé,
Rends-moi le Pausilippe et la mer d'Italie,
La *fleur* qui plaisait tant à mon cœur désolé,
Et la treille où le pampre à la rose s'allie.

Suis-je Amour ou Phébus? . . . Lusignan ou Biron?
Mon front est rouge encor du baiser de la reine;
J'ai rêvé dans la grotte où nage la syrène . . .

Et j'ai deux fois vainqueur traversé l'Achéron:
Modulant tour à tour sur la lyre d'Orphée
Les soupirs de la sainte et les cris de la fée.

El Desdichado

I am the shadowed—the bereaved—the unconsoled,
The Aquitainian prince of the stricken tower:
My one *star*'s dead, and my constellated lute
Bears the *Black Sun* of *Melancholia*.

You who consoled me, in the tombstone night,
Bring back my Posilipo, the Italian sea,
The *flower* that so pleased my wasted heart,
And the arbour where the vine and rose agree.

Am I Love or Apollo? . . . Lusignan or Biron?
My brow is red still from the kiss of the queen;
I've dreamed in the cavern where the siren swims . . .

And twice a conqueror have crossed Acheron:
Modulating on the Orphic lyre in turn
The sighs of the saint, and the fairy's screams.

Myrtho

Je pense à toi, Myrtho, divine enchanteresse,
Au Pausilippe altier, de mille feux brillant,
A ton front inondé des clartés d'Orient,
Aux raisins noirs mêlés avec l'or de ta tresse.

C'est dans ta coupe aussi que j'avais bu l'ivresse,
Et dans l'éclair furtif de ton œil souriant,
Quand aux pieds d'Iacchus on me voyait priant,
Car la Muse m'a fait l'un des fils de la Grèce.

Je sais pourquoi là-bas le volcan s'est rouvert ...
C'est qu'hier tu l'avais touché d'un pied agile,
Et de cendres soudain l'horizon s'est couvert.

Depuis qu'un duc normand brisa tes dieux d'argile,
Toujours, sous les rameaux du laurier de Virgile,
La pâle Hortensia s'unit au Myrthe vert!

Myrtho

I ponder you, Myrtho, divine enchantress,
Proud Posilipo, a million fires ablaze,
Your forehead in a flood of Eastern rays,
Your braids of gold entangled with black grapes.

In your cup too I tasted drunkenness,
And in the furtive lightning of your smile
Seeing me at the feet of Bacchus kneel,
For the Muse elected me a son of Greece.

I know why that volcano stirs again:
Your light foot touched it only yesterday,
And suddenly ash blanketed the sky.

Since a Norman duke shattered your gods of clay,
Always, beneath the boughs of Vergil's bay,
The pale Hydrangea meets the Myrtle green!

Horus

Le dieu Kneph en tremblant ébranlait l'univers:
Isis, la mère, alors se leva sur sa couche,
Fit un geste de haine à son époux farouche,
Et l'ardeur d'autrefois brilla dans ses yeux verts.

«Le voyez-vous, dit-elle, il meurt, ce vieux pervers,
Tous les frimas du monde ont passé par sa bouche,
Attachez son pied tors, éteignez son œil louche,
C'est le dieu des volcans et le roi des hivers!

L'aigle a déjà passé, l'esprit nouveau m'appelle,
J'ai revêtu pour lui la robe de Cybèle . . .
C'est l'enfant bien-aimé d'Hermès et d'Osiris!»

La Déesse avait fui sur sa conque dorée,
La mer nous renvoyait son image adorée,
Et les cieux rayonnaient sous l'écharpe d'Iris.

Horus

Trembling, the god Kneph shook the universe:
Then mother Isis rose up on her bed,
Gestured at her savage spouse in hatred,
And the old passion blazed in her green eyes.

"See him?" she said. "He's dying now, that brute,
The frosts of all the world are in his gut;
Put out his squint eye, tie his twisted foot—
He's king of winters, the volcanoes' god!

The eagle's flown: I hear the new spirit call—
I have put on Cybele's gown once more,
For Hermes' and Osiris's dear son!"

The Goddess vanished on her golden shell.
The sea sent back her image we revere;
Under the scarf of Iris the heavens shone.

Antéros

Tu demandes pourquoi j'ai tant de rage au cœur
Et sur un col flexible une tête indomptée;
C'est que je suis issu de la race d'Antée,
Je retourne les dards contre le dieu vainqueur.

Oui, je suis de ceux-là qu'inspire le Vengeur,
Il m'a marqué le front de sa lèvre irritée,
Sous la pâleur d'Abel, hélas! ensanglantée,
J'ai parfois de Caïn l'implacable rougeur!

Jéhovah! le dernier, vaincu par ton génie,
Qui, du fond des enfers, criait: «O tyrannie!»
C'est mon aïeul Bélus ou mon père Dagon . . .

Ils m'ont plongé trois fois dans les eaux du Cocyte,
Et protégeant tout seul ma mère Amalécyte,
Je ressème à ses pieds les dents du vieux dragon.

Anteros

You ask why I have so much rage at heart
And an untamed head upon a pliant neck;
As a descendant of Antæan stock
I throw the spears back at the conquering god.

Yes, I am one of those the Avenger fires,
He marked my forehead with his angry mouth,
At times I've Cain's relentless flush beneath
The pallor of poor Abel's bloodstained face.

Jehovah! The last who by your spirit fell
And shouted "Tyrant!" from the pit of hell
Was Baal my forebear or my father Dagon . . .

They plunged me in Cocytus three times. Now
My Amálekite mother's only guard, I sow
Again at her feet the teeth of the old dragon.

Delfica

La connais-tu, DAFNÉ, cette ancienne romance,
Au pied du sycomore, ou sous les lauriers blancs,
Sous l'olivier, le myrthe ou les saules tremblants,
Cette chanson d'amour . . . qui toujours recommence!

Reconnais-tu le TEMPLE, au péristyle immense,
Et les citrons amers où s'imprimaient tes dents?
Et la grotte, fatale aux hôtes imprudents,
Où du dragon vaincu dort l'antique semence.

Ils reviendront ces dieux que tu pleures toujours!
Le temps va ramener l'ordre des anciens jours;
La terre a tressailli d'un souffle prophétique . . .

Cependant la sibylle au visage latin
Est endormie encor sous l'arc de Constantin:
—Et rien n'a dérangé le sévère portique.

Delphica

Do you recognize, DAPHNE, the old refrain,
At the sycamore's foot, by the white laurels, below
The olive, myrtle or the trembling willow,
The love-song . . . always starting up again!

Remember the TEMPLE, its endless colonnade,
The bitter lemons printed with your teeth?
And, fatal to rash visitors, the cave
Where sleeps the conquered dragon's ancient seed.

They will come back, those gods you always mourn!
Time will return the order of old days;
The land has shivered with prophetic breath . . .

Meanwhile the Sibyl with the latin face
Still sleeps beneath the arch of Constantine:
—And nothing has disturbed the austere porch.

Artémis

La Treizième revient ... C'est encor la première;
Et c'est toujours la seule,—ou c'est le seul moment:
Car es-tu reine, ô toi! la première ou dernière?
Es-tu roi, toi le seul ou le dernier amant? ...

Aimez qui vous aima du berceau dans la bière;
Celle que j'aimai seul m'aime encor tendrement:
C'est la mort—ou la morte ... O délice! ô tourment!
La rose qu'elle tient, c'est la *Rose trémière*.

Sainte napolitaine aux mains pleines de feux,
Rose au cœur violet, fleur de sainte Gudule:
As-tu trouvé ta croix dans le désert des cieux?

Roses blanches, tombez! vous insultez nos dieux:
Tombez fantômes blancs de votre ciel qui brûle:
—La sainte de l'abîme est plus sainte à mes yeux!

Artemis

The Thirteenth comes back . . . is again the first,
And always the only one—or the only time:
Are you then queen, O you! the first or last?
You, the one or last lover, are you king? . . .

Love who loved you from the cradle to the hearse.
Alone my love still loves me tenderly,
She is death—or the dead one . . . Torment! Joy!
The rose she carries is the *Mallow* rose.

Neapolitan saint with your hands full of fire,
Rose with the violet heart, St Gudula's flower,
In heaven's desert have you found your cross?

White roses, fall! You insult our gods:
Fall, white phantoms, from your burning skies:
—The saint of the pit is holier in my eyes!

Le Christ aux Oliviers

Dieu est mort! le ciel est vide . . .
Pleurez! enfants, vous n'avez plus de père!
JEAN PAUL

I

Quand le Seigneur, levant au ciel ses maigres bras,
Sous les arbres sacrés, comme font les poètes,
Se fut longtemps perdu dans ses douleurs muettes,
Et se jugea trahi par des amis ingrats;

Il se tourna vers ceux qui l'attendaient en bas
Rêvant d'être des rois, des sages, des prophètes . . .
Mais engourdis, perdus dans le sommeil des bêtes,
Et se prit à crier: «Non, Dieu n'existe pas!»

Ils dormaient. «Mes amis, savez-vous *la nouvelle?*
J'ai touché de mon front à la voûte éternelle;
Je suis sanglant, brisé, souffrant pour bien des jours!

Frères, je vous trompais: Abîme! abîme! abîme!
Le dieu manque à l'autel, où je suis la victime . . .
Dieu n'est pas! Dieu n'est plus!» Mais ils dormaient
    toujours!

Christd on the Mount of Olives

God is dead! The heavens are empty . . .
Weep, children, you no longer have a father!
JEAN PAUL RICHTER

I

When the Lord raised his thin arms to the skies
Beneath the sacred trees, as poets do,
Long lost in speechless agonies, and knew
Himself betrayed by thankless friends, to those

Attending him below he turned, those lost
Numb in the sleep of beasts, or in their dreams
Of being sages, prophets, or great kings . . .
And started shouting, "God does not exist!"

They slept. "*The change*, friends—can you see it now?
I've touched the eternal firmament with my brow;
I've suffered many days, bleeding, broken!

Brothers, I cheated you: Abyss, abyss!
God's missing from my altar of sacrifice . . .
There is no God! No God now!" They slept on.

II

Il reprit: «Tout est mort! J'ai parcouru les mondes;
Et j'ai perdu mon vol dans leurs chemins lactés,
Aussi loin que la vie, en ses veines fécondes,
Répand des sables d'or et des flots argentés:

Partout le sol désert côtoyé par des ondes,
Des tourbillons confus d'océans agités . . .
Un souffle vague émeut les sphères vagabondes,
Mais nul esprit n'existe en ces immensités.

En cherchant l'œil de Dieu, je n'ai vu qu'un orbite
Vaste, noir et sans fond; d'où la nuit qui l'habite
Rayonne sur le monde et s'épaissit toujours;

Un arc-en-ciel étrange entoure ce puits sombre,
Seuil de l'ancien chaos dont le néant est l'ombre,
Spirale, engloutissant les Mondes et les Jours!

II

He went on, "All is dead! I've passed through worlds;
I've lost my flight among their milky paths,
As far as life in fertile veins unfolds
The golden sands and floods of silver waves:

Everywhere waters coast the desert earth,
Bewildered swirls of agitated seas . . .
The wandering spheres are moved by some vague breath,
But there's no spirit in those vastnesses.

I looked for God's eye, only saw a black
Bottomless socket pouring out its dark
Night on the world in ever thickening rays;

A weird rainbow circles that grim pit,
Brink of old chaos, nothingness its shade,
A spiral swallowing the Worlds and Days!

III

«Immobile Destin, muette sentinelle,
Froide Nécessité! . . . Hasard qui t'avançant,
Parmi les mondes morts sous la neige éternelle,
Refroidis, par degrés l'univers pâlissant,

Sais-tu ce que tu fais, puissance originelle,
De tes soleils éteints, l'un l'autre se froissant . . .
Es-tu sûr de transmettre une haleine immortelle,
Entre un monde qui meurt et l'autre renaissant? . . .

O mon père! est-ce toi que je sens en moi-même?
As-tu pouvoir de vivre et de vaincre la mort?
Aurais-tu succombé sous un dernier effort

De cet ange des nuits que frappa l'anathème . . .
Car je me sens tout seul à pleurer et souffrir,
Hélas! et si je meurs, c'est que tout va mourir!»

III

"Motionless Destiny, dumb sentry, cold
Necessity! . . . Chance, as you range across
Dead worlds forever in the hold of snow,
And slowly freeze the paling universe,

Primordial power, do you comprehend,
Now that your suns consume and crush to death,
What you are doing? Can you surely send
From dying to renascent worlds life's breath?

Father! Within me, is it you I feel?
Have you the strength to live and conquer death?
Or will the outcast angel of the night

Have overturned you with his final thrust?
I am alone in suffering and grief,
And if I die, it's death to everything!"

IV

Nul n'entendait gémir l'éternelle victime,
Livrant au monde en vain tout son cœur épanché;
Mais prêt à défaillir et sans force penché,
Il appela le *seul*—éveillé dans Solyme:

«Judas! lui cria-t-il, tu sais ce qu'on m'estime,
Hâte-toi de me vendre, et finis ce marché:
Je suis souffrant, ami! sur la terre couché . . .
Viens! ô toi qui, du moins, as la force du crime!»

Mais Judas s'en allait mécontent et pensif,
Se trouvant mal payé, plein d'un remords si vif
Qu'il lisait ses noirceurs sur tous les murs écrites . . .

Enfin Pilate seul, qui veillait pour César,
Sentant quelque pitié, se tourna par hasard:
«Allez chercher ce fou!» dit-il aux satellites.

IV

No one heard the eternal victim groan,
Yielding his full heart to the world in vain;
But slumped in feebleness, about to faint
He called to the *one*—awake in Jerusalem:

"Judas!" he shouted, "Sell me, don't waste time
Getting the deal done; you know what I'm worth:
I suffer here, friend, lying on the earth,
Come! For at least you have the strength of crime."

Judas was leaving, vexed and pensive, full
(Though he felt badly paid) of such keen shame
He read his foulness written on each wall . . .

Pilate alone, who ruled in Caesar's name,
Feeling some pity, turned at last by chance:
"Go, find this lunatic!" he told his servants.

V

C'était bien lui, ce fou, cet insensé sublime . . .
Cet Icare oublié qui remontait les cieux,
Ce Phaéton perdu sous la foudre des dieux,
Ce bel Atys meurtri que Cybèle ranime!

L'augure interrogeait le flanc de la victime,
La terre s'enivrait de ce sang précieux . . .
L'univers étourdi penchait sur ses essieux,
Et l'Olympe un instant chancela vers l'abîme.

«Réponds! criait César à Jupiter Ammon,
Quel est ce nouveau dieu qu'on impose à la terre?
Et si ce n'est un dieu, c'est au moins un démon . . . »

Mais l'oracle invoqué pour jamais dut se taire;
Un seul pouvait au monde expliquer ce mystère:
—Celui qui donna l'âme aux enfants du limon.

V

Yes, it was he, the exalted lunatic . . .
The forgotten Icarus who flew again,
Phaëthon lost in thunderbolts, the slain
Young Attis whom Cybele resurrects!

They scanned the entrails of the sacrifice,
The earth was drunk with that most precious blood . . .
The universe swayed on its axle, stunned,
Olympus reeled a moment toward the abyss.

Invoking Jupiter Ammon, Caesar cried,
"Who is this new god foisted on the world?
Answer! A devil, if he's not a god . . . "

But the oracle stayed silent from that day.
One only could explain this mystery:
He who gave a soul to the sons of clay.

Vers Dorés

Eh quoi! tout est sensible!
PYTHAGORE

Homme, libre penseur! te crois-tu seul pensant
Dans ce monde où la vie éclate en toute chose?
Des forces que tu tiens ta liberté dispose,
Mais de tous tes conseils l'univers est absent.

Respecte dans la bête un esprit agissant:
Chaque fleur est une âme à la Nature éclose;
Un mystère d'amour dans le métal repose;
«Tout est sensible!» Et tout sur ton être est puissant.

Crains, dans le mur aveugle, un regard qui t'épie:
A la matière même un verbe est attaché . . .
Ne la fais pas servir à quelque usage impie!

Souvent dans l'être obscur habite un Dieu caché;
Et comme un œil naissant couvert par ses paupières,
Un pur esprit s'accroît sous l'écorce des pierres!

Golden Lines

So then – all things feel!
PYTHAGORAS

Do you believe that thought, free-thinking Man,
Is yours alone in this world that bursts with life?
Your liberty controls the powers you have,
But the universe is absent from your plan.

Respect in animals an active mind:
Each flower to Nature is a blossomed soul;
A mystery of love inhabits metal;
"All things feel!" And all sway humankind.

Beware the blind wall with its watchful gaze:
Tied to the heart of matter is a word . . .
Make matter serve no use that's impious!

Often a God lives in obscure things hid;
And like an eye at birth veiled by its lid,
Under the skin of stones a pure soul grows!

Biographical Note

GÉRARD DE NERVAL was born Gérard Labrunie in Paris on 22 May 1808. His mother died when he was two. In his father's absence as a military surgeon serving the Grande Armée of Napoleon, he was brought up by his mother's uncle in the Valois until his father returned when he was six. At school in Paris, where Latin, Greek and French history were his main subjects, he met Théophile Gautier who became a lifelong friend. His early reputation as a writer came with the publication in 1828 of his translation of Goethe's *Faust* (Part One), and in 1830 of his *Choix de poésies allemandes*. After brief attempts to study law and medicine, he became a literary journalist and freelance writer; he collaborated on plays with Dumas and others, fell in love with the actress Jenny Colon, and spent most of an inheritance on a short-lived theatre magazine which he founded in 1835. He was a leading member of the Jeunes–France movement, renowned for his eccentricity and charm, his love of folklore, legends and occult mythology.

At various times he travelled abroad, notably to Italy, Austria, Egypt, Palestine and Turkey. His *Voyage en Orient* appeared in final book form in 1851. Always on the breadline, he was much loved and respected by his contemporaries such as Gautier, Dumas, Méry and Houssaye; despite his father's strong disapproval of his irregular way of life, Gérard dined with him regularly on Thursday evenings. He frequently returned to haunt the scenes of his childhood round the forests and lakes of Chantilly.

His first breakdown happened in 1841. From then until his suicide he was intermittently treated by Dr Esprit Blanche and his son Emile at their famous clinic in Paris, first at Montmartre and later in Passy. Dr Emile Blanche, who befriended him, gave him the use of an attic room as a study overlooking the large garden at the Passy clinic, where during 1853–4 he worked on the autobiographic *Aurélia* and supervised the publication of his collected writings. *Les Filles du Feu*, including his prose masterpiece *Sylvie* and the sonnet-sequence *Les Chimères*, appeared early in 1854.

After a trip to Germany he returned to Passy, but discharged himself against Dr Blanche's advice in October. For the last few weeks of his life he was homeless, living in lodging-houses and "spikes", and writing in public libraries and cheap cafés. On 25 January 1855, he wrote a letter to his aunt which ended, "Don't expect me this evening, for the night will be black and white." At dawn the next day he was found hanged from a grating at the foot of the stone steps in the snow-covered rue de la Vieille-Lanterne.

A Letter on a Line by Nerval
RICHARD HOLMES

Valois, May 1984

Dear Peter,

I have just got back from a walk in the park at Ermenon-
ville with Sophie. The gates were locked, but we climbed
over a spiked grill. The château has been taken over by the
Hare Krishna sect since 1981—there were faded graffiti
on the wall near the church, *Oui à Rousseau, oui à Nerval,
non à Krishna*—but the rest is unchanged. We saw the long
lake with its chestnut trees, their white candles growing
right down to the water's surface; Jean-Jacques's grey
stone tomb on the little island, surrounded by poplars
(Sophie wanted to swim out to it); and we even found the
small broken temple, with its half-circle of columns,
hidden in the bushes high up on the promontory above,
which Nerval describes so hauntingly in *Sylvie*, and which I
have always thought of as the gateway into the *Chimères*,
because of its associations.

Nerval wrote: "It takes the same form as the Temple of
the Sibyl at Tivoli . . . the unfinished building is already
little more than a ruin, gracefully festooned with ivy, its
uneven steps overgrown by brambles. It was here, when
just a child, that I saw the festivals where the local girls
dressed in white and came up to receive their prizes for
schoolwork or good conduct. Where are the climbing roses
that used to encircle the hill? The eglantine and the
raspberry bushes have overrun the last of their beds, which
are reverting to their wild state. As for the laurels, have
they been cut down—as in the folksong of the little girls
who don't want to play in the woods anymore? No, those
shrubs from the warm land of Italy have died out under our
misty skies. Happily the privet bush, sacred to Vergil, still
flourishes, as if to support the words of the master carved

above the temple door: *Rerum cognoscere causas!* Yes, this temple like so many others is falling down; people become forgetful or weary and turn away from its precincts; and indifferent nature reclaims the ground taken from her by art. But the thirst for knowledge remains eternal, the spring of all action and every power!"

The Vergilian inscription is still there, incomplete around the moss-covered peristyle: "happy is he who shall discover the cause of things". We sat on the steps and rolled a cigarette. Sophie suddenly laughed: "But is it true, what he says? Sometimes the cause of things is much better left alone, in the dark, where it is happy." (I can never translate Sophie's lovely direct way of talking.) It set me thinking again of the *Chimères*, all those delicate problems of rendering the verse into English you have had, and the difficulty of explaining exactly what they mean. Perhaps they are better left alone, in the dark, so the spell isn't broken, as Nerval once said. Perhaps one shouldn't try to know their *causa*. Translate, but don't interpret? I wonder.

In some ways Nerval's poetry is so simple. Simple grammar, simple vocabulary, a series of clear sharp images. There's none of those shifting smoky abstractions of Mallarmé; none of Baudelaire's ironic posing (I always imagine him at a café table showing a lot of shirt-cuff). Nerval by comparison is almost *naïf*, a sort of Douanier Rousseau. So many of his lines are like pictures. *Le prince d'Aquitaine à la tour abolie.—La Déesse avait fui sur sa conque dorée.—Sainte napolitaine aux mains pleines de feux.* No wonder he liked the Tarot cards, with their bold thick outlines, and their emblematic meanings. In fact sometimes I imagine the *Chimères* like a pack of cards—seven sonnets, that's 98 lines or cards—which you can shuffle and rearrange to find new combinations or suits of meaning. But the thing is to get the royal straight flush. (I'm not counting the "Oliviers" sonnets, those five are sacred ones with their own clear religious logic; while these

LA·MAISON·DIEV

L'ÉTOILE

seven are profane and occult in their mysterious meaning.) You could almost consult them for divinations—but I suppose that's more like the *I Ching*. Their basic materials are very like fortune telling or astrology, all the same: Love, Happiness, Misfortune, the Favour or Anger of the Gods, Memory, Desire, Madness, Death, the Hope of Rebirth. It's one of the reasons I always go back to them, hoping for a better deal.

But their meaning, their *causa*, in a more strict literary sense, is not so simple. Can one ever interpret all their mythology, all their secret biographical references, all their cries of anguish and delight? Sophie would probably say such an attempt was itself meaningless, a sort of stupidity (like locking up a park). But I thought I might try to explain, to interpret, just *one* line, and we'll see if that makes us happy. It's the sixth line from "Delfica", the one sonnet, incidentally, to which Nerval gave a precise date and place of composition—Tivoli, 1843—which links it of course to the temple at Ermenonville. (Needless to say Gérard was almost certainly never at Tivoli in 1843.) The line has always fascinated me, and I have thought about it for years. It's got no mythic figure, no Tarot reference. It simply describes the action of an unnamed woman, the beloved:

> *Et les citrons amers où s'imprimaient tes dents*
> [And the bitter lemons bitten/printed/punctured by your teeth]

Leaving aside the premonition of Lawrence Durrell—*Bitter Lemons*—on Cyprus (perhaps not so irrelevant, for Cyprus was the birthplace of Venus and this is clearly a line of amorous longing in some form), the image arrives with a clean, sharp physical impact. You can almost taste it. You can certainly hear it, with its sudden little moaning rhyme, coming unexpectedly from the inside (but invisible to the naked English eye!)—*citrons/dents*. But the sensation is complicated—bitterness and lusciousness combined, desire and regret. And immediately one suspects a "Proustian device", one of those physical actions (so often involving the mouth—the toast dipped in tea, or the famous madeleine cake) which sets off a whole chain reaction of memories. In fact Proust admits in *Contre Sainte-Beuve* that he first discovered this technique in Nerval. The lover's mouth closes on the lemon, with a little flash of bright pearly teeth—yes, you'd remember it!

But the lemons and the teeth are also symbolic objects. That is one of the first principles of the *Chimères*. Everything stands for, or conjures up, something or someone else. (Which is why, presumably, *messieurs les critiques littéraires* call Nerval one of the fathers of the Symbolist Movement—but that is a question for Symons or Rinsler.) So what can one make of the symbolism?

Nerval's lemons represent, I think, the powers of life and healing. In folklore, the lemon is sometimes the original of the fruit of the Tree of Knowledge; and in folk medicine its bitter astringent taste is considered therapeutic. There are all kinds of common associations. Lemons were given to sailors against scurvy (the blessed Vit. C), and they are often eaten with seafood, *les fruits de mer* including the aphrodisiac oyster, as well as being taken with those other restoratives, black tea and rum. More generally, the bitterness and sharpness of the lemon expresses the shock of material reality and lived experience, as against the sweet honeyed illusions of dreams and fantasy.

Does this sound a bit far-fetched? Well, I can quote Gérard himself on the subject, again from *Sylvie*, in a passage that also bears on the symbolic movement of the poems as a whole. "Such are the chimeras," he says, "which charm and lead us astray in the morning of life. . . . The illusions fall away, one after another, like the peel of fruit; and the fruit itself is the experience. Its taste is bitter [*amer*]; but it has something astringent [*âcre*] about it, which fortifies us. . . . " This lemon-like bitterness of experience and memory, combined or contrasted with its astringent revivifying power, continually appears in the imagery and the poet's reactions—"O délice! ô tourment!" ("Artémis"). It is particularly evident in the contrasted pairs of plants or fruit or flowers he uses everywhere—the romantic pallor of the hydrangea, for example, uniting with the robust evergreen myrtle in "Myrtho".

Nerval loved this silent, beautiful world of plants—the description of Ermenonville is full of it—and no less than five out of those seven sonnets have this powerful vegetable life—so to speak—reaching their apotheosis (that's the right word, because they become godlike) in "Vers Dorés". The poems are richly planted out with climbing roses, olive trees, laurels, sycamores, myrtles, and in fact they form a kind of magic landscape, a landscape of the southern Mediterranean, of Italy and Greece, where Nerval had travelled. They create a curiously convincing sense of place, a *genius loci*, semi-classical, a landscape half-seen and half-dreamed (or remembered from a dream) rather like the paintings of Claude Lorrain. (There was a marvellous exhibition of Claude last year at the Grand-Palais; you could see why all the British and French Romantics loved him, his hovering golden dusks with small groups of classical figures—gods or heroes—getting into boats or hanging about in ruined temples.) Ten years after Nerval's death, Corot was painting his dream landscapes like the "Souvenir de Mortefontaine".

But the landscapes of the *Chimères* belong to the countryside round Naples, which Gérard visited twice, in 1834 and 1843. The clifftops of the Posilipo, the grotto of Cumae, the temples of Herculaneum and Pompeii, the slumbering volcano of Vesuvius, and the glittering sea of the bay of Naples. . . . There are biographical reasons for this, but also an important literary one. For Nerval, this was Vergil's country. Vergil's tomb stands beneath a laurel tree on the hillside of Posilipo overlooking the sea (in "El Desdichado", "Myrtho", "Delfica" and "Artémis"). The prophetic Sibyl—*la sibylle au visage latin*—guided Vergil's Aeneas through the underworld, a journey of intense significance to Nerval, who described his own madness as "that which, for the ancients, was represented by the idea of a descent into the infernal regions" (*Aurélia*). He also thought of Vergil, typically, in the medieval occult way, as a kind of poet-magician—a Mage whose poetry had divinatory powers—and who provided a path, or a charm maybe, through the subterranean regions of the mind. This underworld of caves, grottoes, and waters of Lethe (or Cocytus), gives much of the darkness and terror to the landscape of the *Chimères*.

The landscape, which bears the lemon as one symbol of

healing and renewing powers in nature, also bears Vergil's poetry as a symbol of renewal and metaphysical healing in art. Particularly, it bears Vergil's Fourth Eclogue. In the first printing of "Delfica", in *L'Artiste* of 1845, Nerval explicitly placed a line from the Eclogue as his epigraph: *Ultima Cumaei venit iam carminis aetas.* . . . "Now comes the Last Age, according to the oracle at Cumae; the great cycle of lifetimes starts anew; now the virgin goddess returns. . . . "

This famous poem predicts the return of some wonderful Golden Age, a new paradise on earth, heralded by the birth—or is it rebirth?—of a child; and the return also of the ancient gods and goddesses in a new incarnation. It was much loved by the Romantics, and Shelley gave the Eclogue a revolutionary meaning in his chorus from *Hellas* (1822), "The world's great age begins anew. . . . " Nerval interprets it more spiritually, even theologically, in the *Chimères*; and in "Delfica" it has a heart-rending, tearful longing to it, for the beloved woman seems to associate her own fate with those of the old gods. She can only return, if they return. *Ils reviendront ces dieux que tu pleures toujours! / Le temps va ramener l'ordre des anciens jours.* Why this should be is not immediately clear. But Nerval obviously associates the return of the Golden Age, the redeeming of time, and of love perhaps, with the return of the lady who bit into the lemons.

Et les citrons amers où s'imprimaient tes dents

So much for the lemons; what of the teeth? Once again their symbolic associations are rich. In folklore, as also in dreams, teeth are usually some kind of talisman, linked with luck and fortune, and especially with the sexual appetite. Biting into the lemon is symbolically a sexual act—both passionate and devouring; so the teeth flash in the moment of orgasm, and the lover promises to eat you up, darling. In "Delfica" biting the lemon suggests the beloved's eagerness for life and experience, so that she seems both innocent and profoundly knowing in the act. Her bright teeth bite into the rough, pungent rind, tasting the *zest*, both delicately penetrating and confidently taking possession.

But these pearly teeth, like everything else in the *Chimères*, also have their mythological meaning, which is altogether more primitive. They are explicitly linked with the famous dragon's teeth, *les dents du vieux dragon* in "Antéros" which become *l'antique semence* of the dragon in "Delfica". These are the seed-teeth which the goddess Athene ordered Cadmus to sow; they sprang up as warriors who helped to found the great city of Thebes (Ovid tells the rest of the story in *Metamorphoses* Book 3). So these teeth are also magic seeds, with an ancient fructifying power, and they too partake of the whole process of struggle and renewal—burial and rebirth, destruction and creation—which is celebrated in the sonnets; but they emphasize the defiant aspect.

This weaving in of classical mythology (from Ovid, or Vergil) is characteristic of the *Chimères*, so that figures such as Orpheus, Antaeus, and Iris flicker up through its lines, like the royal cards appearing in the pack. *Car la Muse*, wrote Nerval, *m'a fait l'un des fils de la Grèce* ("Myrtho"). But not only Greece.

The poems also use older, pre-classical systems, and particularly those of Egypt and the Nile, where Nerval had also travelled in the summer of 1843, visiting Cairo, Alexandria and the Pyramids. These appear most explicitly in "Horus", which re-enacts the myth of the goddess Isis and her son-lover Osiris, who rebel against the paternal tyranny of Kneph (a god of war like Vulcan, and crippled like Nerval's own father). But the seasonal fertility myths of Isis, associated with river-floodings, the sea and the moon, run subtly throughout the poems.

This palimpsest of mythologies (is that a B-movie word,

conjuring up *The Curse of the Mummy's Tomb?*) reflects Nerval's lifelong fascination with what we should now call comparative religion. He once claimed, while leaning against the fireplace in Victor Hugo's *salon* in the Place Royale—now the Place des Vosges, with its lime trees—to have "seventeen religions, seventeen religions at least." (I always loved this story—told by Gautier—a perfect example of *le bon Gérard*'s slightly mischievous humour.) He wrote a brilliant and pioneering essay on the archetypal elements in French folklore and country superstitions in *Chansons et Legendes du Valois*. He also sketched out a theory in his essay "Isis", one of *Les Filles du Feu*, that Classical and Egyptian mythology combined to produce many of the doctrines of Christianity—in particular the Biblical idea of the Garden of Eden (or Golden Age), the resurrection of Christ (Osiris and the fertility gods of the Nile), and the mediating role of the Virgin Mary (Isis, or the Mother Goddess). The passionate hope that modern man may somehow return to the springs of such religious beliefs, and that *l'antique semence* may bear fruit again, and redeem a materialistic world, gives much of its poignancy to "Delfica", and is one of the master themes of the *Chimères*.

There are of course several other magical or mythological systems of reference at work in the poems. The symbolism of the Tarot cards is one (especially in "El Desdichado", and "Artémis"); the seven mystic processes of Alchemy is another; and the pre-analytical medical psychology which Nerval encountered during his long stays in Dr Blanche's asylum at Passy, is a third. Those plunges into the waters of Lethe or Cocytus ("Antéros") make a mournful reference to the therapeutic technique of immersing delirious or hysterical patients in baths of freezing water, a crude forerunner of later electric-shock treatment. Several of these episodes are described in *Aurélia* in terms that directly relate to the imagery of the

Chimères, and show the mythologizing process at work as part of Gérard's defence of his own identity against the onslaughts of insanity.

"I felt myself plunged into cold water, and even colder water streaming over my forehead. I fixed my thoughts on the eternal Isis, the mother goddess and the sacred spouse. All my yearning, all my prayers were concentrated in that magic name, I felt myself coming alive again in her, and sometimes she appeared to me in the form of the classical Venus, and sometimes in the guise of the Christian Virgin. The night brought back this cherished vision more clearly to me, and yet I asked myself: 'What can she do for her poor children, being herself subjected and perhaps persecuted?' Pale and torn, the crescent of the moon grew thinner each evening, and would soon disappear: perhaps we should never see her again in the sky! Yet it seemed to me that this heavenly planet was the refuge of all my sister souls, and I saw her peopled with plaintive shadows, destined to be reborn one day upon the earth. . . . " A sad, wonderful passage!

I've already said that the beloved woman who bit into the lemons seems to me linked with the return of the Golden Age. But I also think she was simultaneously a real woman, and the goddess Isis in Nerval's memory. Perhaps it's cheating, as far as the poems go, but a look into Nerval's biography and fiction strangely suggests this; and also the way in which he distilled his poetry—a kind of 100° proof moonshine—from carefully stored and treasured (even slightly obsessional) fragments of experience. The first distillation often appears in his letters or newspaper articles; the second distillation in his fiction; and the third—the real firewater—in perhaps a single line of poetry.

I happen to know that there is a letter of Nerval's written to his friend Gautier from Marseilles in November 1834, which first mentions the famous lemons. Gérard was twenty-six years old, and had just returned penniless on the boat from his first visit to Naples, where he had lived "like a tramp". He mentions that his old leather suitcase— "lent me by D'Arc"—was largely empty of provisions except for "one large loaf . . . and two lemons." He also mentions that he had met "a very pretty woman" with a jealous husband, and they had drunk too much champagne together. That's all. But ten years later, he put the boat-crossing from Marseilles to Naples into his story *Octavie* (it went through five versions between 1842 and 1854), and brings the lemons and the woman together in their symbolic role. The narrator of *Octavie* says he met a young English woman, accompanied by her jealous father, bathing in the sea near Marseilles. "Her slender body slid through the green water beside me." (A first hint of her connection with Isis, the water goddess.) Finding her again on the boat to Naples, he fell in love with her.

"The young English woman was on the bridge, pacing up and down with rapid strides. As if impatient with the slow progress of the ship, she bit into the flesh of a lemon with her ivory-white teeth. 'My poor girl,' I exclaimed, 'you are suffering from weak lungs, I am sure, and that is not the medicine you need.' She looked carefully at me and said, 'Whoever told you that?'—'The Sibyl of Tivoli', I replied, unruffled. 'What nonsense, I don't believe a word you are saying.' But she looked at me so tenderly when she said it, that I could not prevent myself from kissing her hand."

Later in the story they meet again at the little temple of Isis at Pompeii, where the narrator intends to declare his love. Instead, he finds himself faithfully explaining all the details of the worship of Isis to her, and they both become strangely entranced. "She suddenly wanted to play the role of the Goddess in the ceremonies, and I found myself charged with the role of Osiris . . . but going back to Naples, and struck by the sublimity of the ideas we had just been acting out, I no longer dared to speak to her of love." So he loses his lady, and she is in some sense transformed into the lost goddess Isis. He's left with nothing but the bitter-sweet memory of her mouth on the lemons. It's the kind of memory—part sexy dream, part sad reality, part pure myth, and part just an aching *nostalgie de pays*—which I think we all recognize, but which Gérard somehow invented first. It should take the name "Nervalian" in English; and never again be confused with "Proustian". It's the difference between silver and purple.

So much for one line of Nerval. Have I really said anything about it at all? Probably not: it still stands there, pristine, powerful, going straight to the heart with a directness that only great poetry has:

Et les citrons amers où s'imprimaient tes dents

I was going to ramble on, comparing it to lines in certain

great English poems which seem to me to have the same qualities, especially that combination of despair and defiant hope which runs throughout the *Chimères*: with Tenny-son's *In Memoriam*, with Eliot's *Waste Land*, with Ted Hughes's *Crow* (that would surprise you!) . . . But luckily Sophie has just come in, bringing fresh-baked bread, *truites roses*, white burgundy and some lemons of course. So I am going out to cut some herbs in the garden—*persil*, *ciboulet, baie*—and a bunch of white lilacs for the table. The moon is coming up over the Marne. I shall make a log fire, as it's quite cold for May.

As ever,

Richard

Translating Nerval: A Reply

PETER JAY

Greenwich, July 1984

Dear Richard,

Belatedly your letter brings me in from the garden, thinking again of you and of Gérard, of how his poems perennially flourish for us both. Your marsh columbines are settling in well, and the hollyhocks which I've raised from seed are now planted out. Sometimes I think they represent the nearest I'll ever come to Nerval, and yet "hollyhocks" sound nothing like "roses trémières" . . . so what do they really have in common?

Once more I've been over the translations, trying to tidy loose ends, hoping here to translate more and interpret less, there to translate less and interpret more . . . above all, tuning each poem, each line, to as Nervalian a "noise" (in Peter Levi's sense) as I can. It's a treacherously difficult business, combining freedom and constraint (restraint?) in ways only those, perhaps, who've tried to get under the skin of foreign poems in order to "English" them can fully understand. "Vers Dorés" could be read as an evocation of the platonic idea of translation—"Under the skin of stones a pure soul grows"; but poetry is as impure as any art form, and translation of poetry is doubly so.

Nerval's practice in his Heine versions was to write the best poetry he could, following the general drift of Heine's lyric movement. I think he was much freer with Heine, who befriended him, than I've dared to be with him, but then I've not been able to visit him and make his acquaintance. Principles in translation are *ad hoc*, they derive from your contact with particular poets or poems; they're the summary of your part-solutions to an individual nexus of problems. Theory is an attempt to codify and evaluate principles from the evidence of many different, often contradictory practices. I've been less methodical than I'd care to admit, were I a scholar or theorist; but I've not yet come across any theoretical precept that's helped me make a line of any translation ring true. In the end, I've had to be "freest" when most awed by the *force majeure* of Nerval's inspiration—but I still maintain that many translators of poetry, whether or not they are poets "in their own right", don't try hard enough to cut to the bone of a poet's words. Liberation can come from sustained meditation on the very words.

The long-acknowledged problem of translation's demand for double loyalties, and the strain it puts on them, has vexed me greatly over the years. It's a classic dilemma, or paradox. Isn't it sometimes like trying to serve two masters—the two languages to which allegiance is owed— or having two concurrent love-affairs? Perhaps it's not often as compromised a performance as that, but simpler analogies with close human relationships are pertinent. I'm thinking of the tensions between lovers with strong personalities who, in striving to pull together, succeed largely in pulling apart. The conscious motivation may be towards principles of balance and fidelity, but the wholly or partially repressed impulse may be to do with possessive control, domination and resistance to subservience. Or desire for it. Don't we talk of "getting into" a poem, of "mastering" or "getting on top of" a passage that seems impenetrable or unyielding, and so on? The metaphors of sexual politics are inevitable. You translate a poet because you're "attracted" to the work, but if the attraction is superficial or false you will be rejected.

Celle que j'aimai seul m'aime encor tendrement

One of those quintessential Nervalian lines, in your sense, utterly simple and memorable, like a rune or a charm. I've found myself repeating it at times, as if to thwart its imagined opposite. An ultimate loyalty is invoked. I've used it as a line for eternal love against the failures of temporal love; for life in the face of everything, against death in the face of nothing. Still I find new resonances in those words. Is the tone of the line accepting and resigned, or can you hear defiance and despair there too?

"We should read whole poets, and always whole poems, yet it is sometimes possible to dislodge the universe with one line." (Peter Levi again, in *The Noise Made by Poems*.) Gérard succeeds in doing so with more lines than almost any poet I know. Apart from lines 3–4 of "El Desdichado", these eruptive lines are all end-stopped, like a self-contained poem within the poem. His great lines astonish you both in and apart from their context—but they never make the rest of the poem fall flat.

Before I had really begun to wrestle with the *Chimères*, my provisional version of that line was: "My only love still loves me tenderly." Your work, and Norma Rinsler's, convinced me of the inadequacy of that as translation, however enamoured of its sound as English I might be. Painfully I struggled through (the surrounding lines were also in flux) to the literal "She I loved alone still loves me tenderly"; then, "She I alone loved loves me tenderly still". Neither are pretty, especially the slurred *she-I-alone*, and neither are rhythmically anything to write home about, but both are fairer to that critical *seul*, even though they still limit its senses. The word is so delicately placed in Gérard's line as to suggest both "she whom I loved when I was alone" and "she whom I was the only person to love".

Tracing the nuances of Nerval's *seul* in these poems is a job for someone. In English you have to juggle with combinations of *only*, *one* and *alone*—*sole* would be an unfortunate homophone—in shifting contexts. Sooner or later you begin to curse the English language for not being French, or French for not being English; and you're right back to the basic conflict of loyalties. Well, I had given up and gone back to "My only love . . .", and we were about to cohabit when I suddenly deserted her for "Alone my love still loves me tenderly". I'm begging this one to make a go of it with me. Fickle? No wonder people talk of abandoning rather than finishing a translation!

Mostly, though, it's been a process of nagging away at the parts which secretly I knew would not quite do, but could see no obvious way to improve. It's ridiculous how long it sometimes takes for the obvious to become clear! Thanks, by the way, for guiding me away from "For the Muse *enrolled* me as a son of Greece." I had to laugh at your "scouts!" in the margin. Less obvious was my dissatisfaction with what I had for:

Je pense à toi, Myrtho, divine enchanteresse . . .

"I think of you, Myrtho, divine enchantress" is accurate and acceptable, and yet when *ponder* presented itself I knew it was what my line needed. As for the contortions I'd put myself through before arriving at the present version of the close of "El Desdichado", you may recall how ingeniously I was contriving, over several years, to avoid a straightforward solution.

Yes, it's a strange and intricate business. It fascinates me. I find translation, at least the translation of poems as rich and deep as those of Gérard, much harder than writing anything of my own, though God knows that's hard enough and I do it all too little. Translating absorbs most of my desire for making verses. But of course this gives me every excuse for writing next to nothing else: perfectionism disguising fear of failure, lack of talent, what have you. In my mellowest moments, I feel that the ultimate necessity of poems is in the lap of the gods. But with other people's poems that have become necessary to *me*, I feel strongly drawn to translate them, to describe and share my sense of their value, hoping (less modestly?) to make them needed in English.

Maybe it's something like that for you, in your bio-graphical-critical work? We could both be said to be writing vicariously, but we don't see ourselves as parasitic, frustrated artists. Why should the jibes like "X is a translator, and it shows" sting? But they do. Perhaps biographers get credit for critical insight, but poetry translators often aren't accorded even that much, and they are generally denied "originality" (that romantic concept, unknown to the sensible ancients) by reviewers who take no interest in their problems.

"But I digress." How much distance one needs from poems, how much closeness to them! I don't think anyone can reconstruct the real reasons for decisions made in the course of a poetic translation, any more than you can describe in sufficient detail the internal course of the choices made in a poem's growth. Even manuscript evidence, I suspect, is misleading: decisions, associative or imaginative leaps, are made *off* the page as often as on it. How to account for one's passions dispassionately? No, I wouldn't believe myself. The danger to avoid is of mounting a critical defence of a translation, with the dubious benefit of hindsight, in the guise of a *methodology*. Actually it's sheer luck, mostly, that leads to those decisive strokes that give you hope that a poem will begin to come good. "Luck" is my word, "inspiration" would be a more traditional way of putting it . . . but the point is that it's unaccountable, finally. I'm as happy as the next person to run the risk of the "intentional fallacy"—we all *have* intentions—but mine with Gérard's poems was mainly to make them convincing in English. What a nerve all that implies!

La rose qu'elle tient, c'est la Rose trémière.

"What was your intention there, M. Nerval?" "*Enfin*, I meant to write an unforgettable line, and to give translators of my poems sleepless nights." Wasn't it you, Richard, who told me that Gérard wrote somewhere to the effect that poetry is what *survives* translation?* Worth remembering for the next time somebody trundles out Frost's definition of poetry as being what is lost in translation. It has a chance of being an equally useful half-truth.

I've rid myself of the etymological fantasy that *rose trémière* has the slightest undercurrent of anything like fear or trembling; and much as we both love hollyhocks, the word as well as the flower, we've agreed that "The rose she's holding is a hollyhock", or near offer, won't do. *Pace* Derek Mahon, of whom more in a moment.

That line, and the poem "Artémis" as a whole, is an extreme example of the delight and torment of verse translation. The strains have told on me here more than anywhere, because to negotiate the extraordinary pressures of this poem, which is the mid-point of *Les Chimères*, translation has to be most strict to be most liberating. Every phrase, every line—so dense, yet so fluid—must be given maximum freedom to let its meanings expand. "What's freedom but the rule of poetry?" is an apposite, if slightly riddling, question to quote in this context.

Derek Mahon's bold idea, starting the poem with "Thirteen o'clock, and the first hour once more", leads you very firmly in the path of one interpretation. By excluding some possibilities, he gives his poem a sharper but a narrower focus. And what about his fifth and sixth lines?

*"Honneur sans doute au rythme et à la rime, caractères primitifs et essentiels de la poésie. Mais ce qu'il y a de plus important, de fondamental, ce qui produit l'impression la plus profonde, ce qui agit avec le plus d'efficacité sur notre moral dans une œuvre poétique, c'est ce qui reste du poète dans une traduction en prose; car cela seul est la valeur réelle de l'étoffe dans sa pureté, dans sa perfection."—Nerval quoting Goethe (from *Dichtung und Wahrheit*) as the authority for his manner of translation, in the 1840 preface to his final version of *Faust*.

The goddess carved on the provincial clock
Of childhood loves you as she always did.

What a fine poet he is! But this looks less like a matter of
making forced choices among ambiguities, than of his
having concluded that Gérard's own choice of words and
images offers no chance of dialogue: so he has compen-
sated by making a fictional Nervalian poem with detail
drawn from the commentaries. There's a fine Odilon
Redon picture of the Ste Gudule clock-tower in Brussels,
which illustrates Mahon's version of Gérard's hidden
allusion; he didn't haul in the clock just for rhyming with
our friends of the *Rosa Althaea* family.

Oddly enough, I was thinking of Derek Mahon in
connexion with Nerval long before I heard that he'd made
a version of *Les Chimères*. (I think of Derek Mahon too
every time I hear birdsong on an empty stomach: "For
who, unbreakfasted, will love the lark?") Along these lines:
if one wanted to imagine the "ideal" translation of *Les
Chimères* in the twentieth century, to what writer in English
would you assign it? Yeats, perhaps?

Not the mystical Yeats of the pernes and gyres, but the
hard-headed, sober Yeats whose touch with pentameters
was so sure, who could write the simple, prosaic bridging
passages as well as the heart-stopping one-liners. Yeats is
not often Nervalian in tone, though: he's both grander—
prone to a strutting magniloquence that the modest Gérard
would never have affected—and, frankly, crazier. In his
writing Nerval is remarkably sane, isn't he? Crazy in a mild
but inoffensive way it may be to take a lobster for a walk on
a lead, but it isn't mad to intimate that lobsters know the
secrets of the deep. (And as you've pointed out, it's an
example of his mischievous sense of humour, too.)

Nerval is far from being a wild romantic. In an age of
excessive gestures, his was not an excessive life-style. In
his writing he puts on no airs and graces, he says exactly

what he has to say as it should be said. Yeats, by contrast, does love to cut an impressive dash. Lines like:

That we descant and yet again descant
Upon the supreme theme of Art and Song

—bellow them in your thickest brogue—spoil for me an otherwise beautiful and moving short poem, "After Long Silence".

If not Yeats, then what other poets have the requisite control and freedom of line? I keep coming back to two of the best poets now writing in traditional forms in England or Ireland: Geoffrey Hill and Derek Mahon. Mahon has been to school with Yeats profitably, and we have his version. I wonder if you will think that he permits himself too much enjambement, making the flow of the poems a little choppy; and that some of his liberties—"My star" for "Ma seule étoile" is one that springs to mind—don't help? But he does make fine sonnets, and that matters. Is Geoffrey Hill, I wonder, moving in the direction of Nerval? That is probably too much to read into his marvellous poem on Charles Péguy.

If you discount the possibility of sonnets in English alexandrines, the whole thing stands or falls on the credibility of a Nervalian pentameter in English. It has to be a clear and supple line, allowing modulation in verbal texture from the plain and relaxed to the compressed (but not muscle-bound). Gérard's lines have such balance, such a fine sense of pace, so little straining for effect. It has to be a line capable of singing, but not in the style of grand opera.

La fleur *qui plaisait tant à mon cœur désolé*

A haunting line, with its unhurried tempo, total economy of means, its poise—look at how he places those internal rhymes, so unobtrusively yet firmly; they seem natural to the language in a quite unstudied way.

I can't get much closer to this. It's something to do with the specific gravity of the verse. How do you measure the moral density of language? Poetry is words in a particular suspension of language, but the only gauge we have is the experience of our ears, and of our hearts. Nothing as scientific as the hydrometer you gave me, which is in regular use for predicting the results of my efforts to turn water into wine (I hope to surprise you with the Italian Classico in October). But in translating, as in any writing, one doesn't proceed by recipes or prescriptions, but by intuition and work; the intuitions often growing out of the work, as if it were the catalyst that causes yeast cells to become active.

Et dans l'éclair furtif de ton œil souriant

Eighteen years have passed since "And in the furtive lightning of your smile" came to me like a gift, promising that one day the rest of *The Chimeras* might grow from it.

And yet there's hardly a line in my version that I don't feel might be bettered, had I but world enough and time. I've gone as far as I can now in entering the Nervalian spirit, but that may not be far enough for the poems. I'd rather swim than sink in them. Returning to less dangerous matters of technique, I've never doubted that a decent version of the *Chimères* has to be in the form of sonnets, tackling them head-on with all the compromises that differences between the state of the French sonnet in the 1840s, and the English sonnet now, must entail. (Poor Gérard was not only plunged in the waters of Cocytus, he has been thrice Californianized, God rest his soul.)

Depending on how you look at it, it was either a natural or a forced decision to use half-rhyme, assonance and other rhyme-substitutes. Compared to French, English is poor in full rhymes, but we also inhabit the last quarter of the twentieth century and must use what comes to hand. Joseph Brodsky, a strict believer in what Dryden called "metaphrase"—extreme literal and formal fidelity, not to say subservience—when it comes to other people's versions of his Russian poems, might consider even this too soft an approach. Do you know his poem "Plato Elaborated"? These lines, in George Kline's version, suddenly struck me as apropos.

> *There would be a café in that city with a quite*
> *decent blancmange, where, if I should ask why*
> *we need the twentieth century when we already*
> *have the nineteenth, my colleague would stare fixedly*
> *at his fork or his knife.*

All the paradoxical questions about the nature and purpose of translation are implicit in those lines. The "impossible" dimension of time-travel, for example . . . and what can I say about the blancmange? Give the poor fellow a spoon!

I still find myself envying Gérard his simplicity and ease of technique, hard-won though I'm convinced it must have been. His poetry *is* inimitable, yet translation is a kind of mimicry. Should I have gone more the way of Robert Lowell, or of Derek Mahon? Did Nerval agonize over such problems in his Heine and other versions, or did he just do the best job he could? Something of the austere, dark ease and compulsion of Geoffrey Hill's technique in his sonnets might have helped me. Yet Hill is more brilliant and more polished than Nerval in some ways, as well as more contorted and self-conscious.

In formal matters, Gérard was not obsessively concerned, for example, to maintain correspondence in his rhyme-schemes from one quatrain to the next, and some of his own rhyming is loose enough. (I say this to encourage myself, *mon brave!*) He could write low-key prosaic lines when they're necessary, which is more often, especially in the "Christ" sequence, than one remembers. The poems don't bombard you with one stunning line after another— he's too good, too sure of his aim, to show off in that way.

It would be worth studying Nerval's enjambements; there are few enough of them, and they're very forceful in "El Desdichado", for instance. I've had to increase their number, especially in narrative passages. English penta-meters lose their rhythmical tension very quickly unless, to apply a famous remark to a different context, the lines are turned across their endings with just the right variation. Defending his use of "English Heroic Verse without Rime", Milton wrote that "true musical delight . . . consists only in apt Numbers, fit quantity of Syllables, and *the sense variously drawn out from one Verse into another*, not in the jingling sound of like endings . . ." (my italics).

It's also a question of rhythmical alertness, and we still have a lot to learn, as some young poets are beginning to realize, from Yeats and Auden. French is a language with a more even distribution of stresses or word-accents than English, which tends to have stronger stresses and is much more monosyllabic. The French alexandrine flows with enough melodic variation, if the poet pays attention—as Gérard always does—to the tone and colour of his interplaying vowels and consonants, and to his variation of pitch. Pitch, of course, is another aspect of language in which French and English habits differ. It's worth remembering that even in "English", pitch is not at all uniform; think of the wildly different cadences of any Irish, Scottish, Welsh or "regional" English poet reading his work aloud. With poets like Heaney, MacDiarmid, Hughes, Harrison or Bunting, to name only a few impressive readers I've heard, pitch is either local or personal, at any rate not "standard". And there must be no less diversity in American English, Caribbean English and so on.

Are English pentameters harder to write well now than alexandrines in French were in the nineteenth century? Is it a relevant question? English alexandrines are a rarity, and they're hardly ever convincing. I remember taking some translation classes at Oxford with the classicist Richmond Lattimore, who died recently. He had published versions of a few Nerval poems.

I am the dark, the widowed, the disconsolate

If only lines as good as that could be sustained!

Here in the midnight of the grave, give back, of late
my consolation, Pausilippe, the Italian
sea, with that flower so sweet once to my desolate
heart, and the trellis where the vine and rose are one.

He's trying for a rapid line with a French sense of light accentuation, but aren't the pentameters crying out to be released? Give or take a few words, like this:

Here in the midnight of the grave, give back,
of late my consolation, Pausilippe, [. . .]
that flower so sweet once to my desolate heart
and the trellis where the vine and rose are one.

English sonnets for French sonnets, sonnet-cycle for sonnet-cycle: the challenge was to anglicize form-and-matter in their integrity. "Tied to the heart of matter is a word . . ./*Ne la fais pas servir à quelque usage impie!*" An injunction to be taken seriously.

I shall have some final, nagging questions of detail to put to you when you're back. (Sorry, but the golden curls have been shorn from "Myrtho"!) And there are questions . . . was Gérard a gardener? Can we find something mystic and Vergilian in Samuel Palmer, or in Turner? By the way, the Corot painting you mentioned is a beauty: let's use that pastoral scene, so evocative of the landscape of Gérard's childhood. I suppose childhood is where it all begins: but that's another story, which I hope you'll get back to telling one day.

A bientôt,
Peter

Select Bibliography of Translations

This list cannot hope to be complete; it notes only those versions which I have chanced across without systematic research. References are to books or anthologies where possible, rather than to periodicals. Peter Hoy has kindly supplemented my list from his records of versions or adaptations published in post-war periodicals. We would be glad to hear of any items which have escaped our attention.

COMPLETE VERSIONS

Robin Blaser, *Les Chimères*, Open Space, San Francisco 1965
Robert Duncan in *Bending the Bow*, New Directions, New York
     1968 (the first printing accidentally omits the last page of the
     "Christ in the Olive Grove" sequence; this is rectified in later
     printings)
Brian Hill in *Fortune's Fool*, Thirty-five Poems by Gérard de
     Nerval, Rupert Hart-Davis, London 1959
Andrew Hoyem, *Chimeras*, Dave Haselwood Books, San
     Francisco 1966
Derek Mahon, *The Chimeras*, Gallery Books, Dublin 1982

PARTIAL VERSIONS

Angel Flores (ed.), *An Anthology of French Poetry from Nerval to
     Valéry in English Translation*, revised edition, Doubleday
     Anchor, New York 1962. Includes versions by Daisy Aldan,
     Barbara Howes and Richmond Lattimore of all seven
     "mystic" poems.
Peter Thompson, "Christ in the Olive Grove", in *Agenda* vol.
     15.4, London 1977–8 (French Poetry Issue).
Geoffrey Wagner in *Selected Writings of Gérard de Nerval*, Peter
     Owen, London 1958. Includes the so-called "Autres
     Chimères" but not "Le Christ aux Oliviers"; the version is
     intended only as a literal.
Rosanna Warren, "Chimères" in *Comparative Criticism* vol. 6,
     Cambridge University Press, 1984. Includes the six poems
     from "El Desdichado" to "Artémis".

INDIVIDUAL POEMS

Versions are surely more numerous than this short list suggests. The earliest translators seem to be Andrew Lang and John Payne. Lang translated only one poem by Nerval, "Fantaisie", in a collection *Ballads and Lyrics of Old France* (1872). Payne in *Flowers of France: the Romantic Period* (The Villon Society, 1906) includes "Christ on Olivet" and "Sonnet" (i.e. "Vers Dorés"), together with ten other Nerval poems. *Les Chimères* attracted no attention, as far as I can see, until after 1945, when Nerval's work underwent a critical revaluation in France.

Martin Bell, adaptation of "El Desdichado" in *Collected Poems 1937–1966*, London 1967

Robert Bly, "Golden Lines" in *The Sixties* no. 5, 1961

John Heath-Stubbs, "El Desdichado" in *Selected Poems*, Oxford 1965

Robert Hellman, "Vers Dorés" in *Mail* no. 3, New York 1970

James Kirkup, "Delfica" and "Myrtho" in *Translation* no. 2, London 1947

Derek Mahon, "The Mute Phenomena" after Nerval (a variation, rather than an adaptation) in *Poems 1962–1978*, Oxford 1979

Irving Ribner, "Le Christ aux Oliviers" in *University of Kansas City Review* vol. 14.3, 1948

W. D. Snodgrass, "El Desdichado" and "Golden Verses" in *After Experience*, London and New York 1968

Andrew Tannahill, Scots version of "The Disinherited" in *Chapman* vol. 3.5, 1975

R. F. Walker, "Allongeons le macaroni" part *c*: "*Les Chimères*, a translittoral" in *The Oxford Literary Review* vol. 2.1, 1977

Edwin Watkins, "El Desdichado" in *Arion* vol. VI.1, Austin, Texas 1967

Richard Wilbur, "Anteros" in *Advice to a Prophet*, New York 1961 and London 1962

Mike Wood, "El Desdichado" in *Granta* vol. LXII no. 1182, Cambridge 1958

David Wright, "Not consolable . . ." in *To the Gods the Shades*, Manchester 1976

Illustrations and Acknowledgements

Frontispiece: photograph of Nerval by Nadar, 1855.
page 8: Albrecht Dürer, "Melencolia I". Engraving, 1514. Art
Institute, Chicago.
page 42: J. M. W. Turner, "The Bay of Baiae, with Apollo and
the Sibyl". Exhibited 1823. The Tate Gallery, London.
pages 44, 51: Cards from a modern Tarot de Marseilles: The
Tower, The Star, The Hanged Man, Death.
page 55: J. M. W. Turner, "Aeneas and the Sibyl, Lake
Avernus". Oil painting, c. 1798–1800. The Tate Gallery,
London.
page 56: Odilon Redon, "A Edgar Poe: 2". Lithograph, 1882.
"Before the black sun of Melancholy, Lenore appears."
page 64: Odilon Redon, lithograph for Le Juré by Edmond
Picard, 1887. "The deep bell of Ste Gudule was tolling the
hour in the belfry nearby."
page 70: Camille Corot, "Souvenir de Mortefontaine". Oil on
canvas, 1864. Musée du Louvre, Paris.
page 74: Odilon Redon, "La Tête d'Orphée (ou Le Noyé)".
Charcoal drawing c. 1885. Rijksmuseum, Amsterdam.

We thank the authors, their representatives and publishers for
permission to quote the following copyright material. The stanza
by Joseph Brodsky from A Part of Speech (1980), Farrar, Straus
and Giroux, New York and Oxford University Press. Lines by
Richmond Lattimore from The Hudson Review, New York,
vol. IV.1 (1951). Derek Mahon and Gallery Books, Dublin for
lines from The Chimeras (1982). The poem by János Pilinszky
from Crater (1978), Anvil Press Poetry. Norma Rinsler and The
Athlone Press, London, for quotations from Les Chimères and
Gérard de Nerval (1973). Our only significant departure from
the French text printed by Norma Rinsler is in the punctuation
of "Delfica", line 9.

Gérard de Nerval

to Zoltán Kocsis

River-bank, that is not river-bank.
Remembrance, that was never sunrise.
Then some kind of water-ditch,
and a burning pin in the head.

JÁNOS PILINSZKY